Stripe Integration in Angular

A Step-by-Step Guide to Creating Payment Functionality

Abdelfattah Ragab

Stripe Integration in Angular

A Step-by-Step Guide to Creating Payment Functionality

Abdelfattah Ragab

Introduction

Welcome to the book "Stripe Integration in Angular: A Step-by-Step Guide to Creating Payment Functionality". In this book, I explain how to integrate Stripe into your Angular application.

Stripe is a leading payment processing platform that enables businesses to accept online payments.

By integrating payment processing into your application, you can create all kinds of e-commerce applications.

You will learn how to create the checkout session, how to use webhooks events and finally how to go live.

By the end of this book, you will be able to process payments in your Angular application and handle all kinds of scenarios.

Let us get started.

What is Stripe?

Stripe is a leading provider of payment services that enables businesses to efficiently accept and process online payments. It enables merchants to process credit and debit card transactions as well as other payment methods via a simple and secure platform. Stripe is particularly popular with start-ups and entrepreneurs as it offers a user-friendly API and robust features that enable quick integration into websites and applications

Create a Stripe account

In order to use Stripe for payment processing, it is necessary to create a Stripe account first. This account serves as the basis for accessing Stripe's services and functions.

Dashboard Management

The Stripe dashboard provides a user-friendly interface where you can manage your payments, view transaction history, process refunds and access analytics. This centralized management is essential for monitoring your company's financial activities.

API Keys

Once you have created an account, you will receive unique API keys that are required to integrate Stripe into your application. These keys authenticate your requests and ensure that your application can communicate securely with Stripe's servers.

Test Mode

Stripe offers a **test mode** that allows you to simulate transactions without processing real payments. This is important for developers to make sure their integration works correctly before it goes live.
You will receive unique API keys for testing that you can use during development.

Going Live

When you're ready for production, simply replace the test API keys with the live API keys. That's it, you don't need to change anything else. You don't need to change anything in the code either. Just replace the test API keys with the live keys and you're done.
For each mode you get two keys, a public one that you can use in your frontend application and a secret one that you should only use in the backend application. Public keys begin with `pk_live_`, while secret keys begin with `sk_live_`.

You'll receive another key pair for testing.
The test keys begin with `pk_test_` and `sk_test_`.

The Backend

To effectively integrate Stripe into an application, both front-end and back-end components are required. Each plays a different role in ensuring secure and efficient payment processing.

The **frontend** is responsible for the user interface through which customers interact with the payment system. It provides users with a seamless and intuitive experience that allows them to enter their payment information and submit transactions easily.

However, the front end alone cannot process payments securely. It must communicate with the backend to complete the transaction.

The **backend** is responsible for the more sensitive aspects of payment processing. It communicates with Stripe's servers using secret API keys that should never be disclosed to the frontend. After the backend receives the response from Stripe, it sends back to the frontend to inform the user of the payment status.

Stripe Payment Process

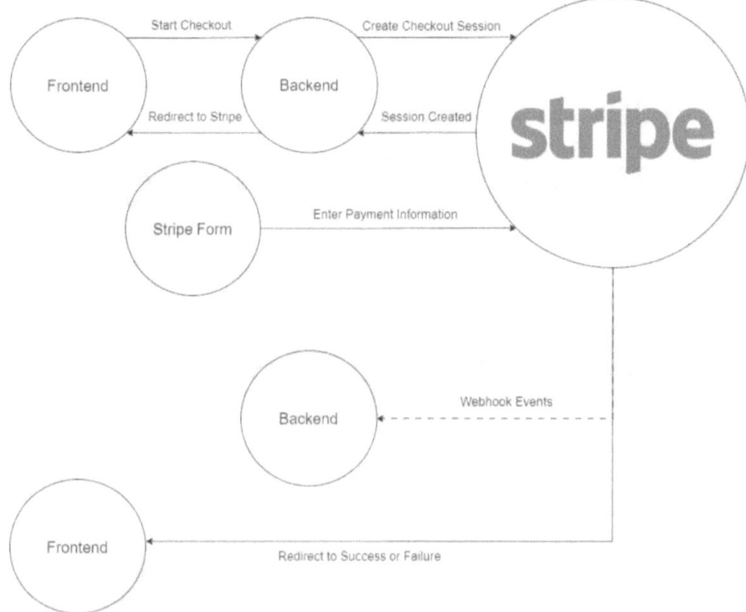

1. When the user clicks the checkout button, we send the items from the shopping cart to the backend and ask it to create a checkout session.
2. It sends it to the Stripe server and asks it to create a checkout session.
3. Stripe creates a session for us and returns its ID.
4. We send this ID to the frontend, which loads the Stripe form for the specified session ID.
5. The user enters their payment details and sends the form to the Stripe server.

6. Stripe informs the backend about webhook events and redirects the frontend accordingly for success or failure.

Practical Example

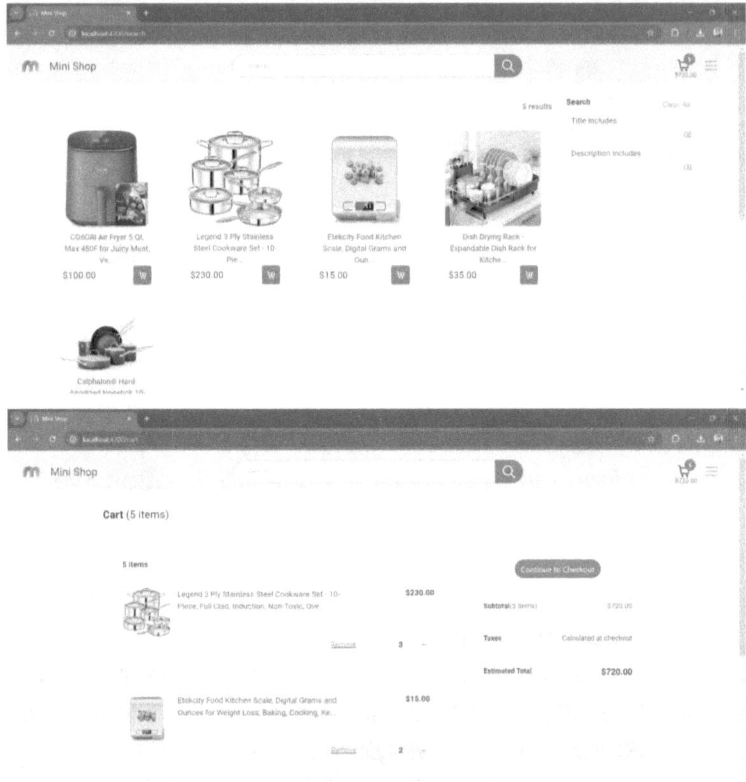

This Angular application consists of two pages, the search page with some products and the shopping cart page.

On the search page, the products are loaded from the backend.
When you click on the "Proceed to checkout" button, nothing happens.
But this will change soon. We will complete the checkout together.
There is another application for the backend that was created with NestJS.
It has two modules for products and orders. We don't connect to the database, we just send an array of products to the frontend.
You can find the code example at
https://books.abdelfattah-ragab.com
Download, unzip and run. Don't forget to `npm install`.
You need to install nest cli on your computer.
To start the Nest application: `nest start`
To start the Angular application: `ng serve`
I will start by working on the backend application.

Debug Enabled

In the Nest application, you can start troubleshooting by clicking on the "Run" menu" → "Start Debugging".
This works because I added a **launch.json** file in the **.vscode** folder. It contains the configuration for NestJS debugging. Simply add this file to any of your NestJS applications to enable debugging.

rawBody

Add both `bodyParser` and `rawBody` to the **main.ts** file. `rawBody` is required for Stripe Webhooks. Activate cors as well. It should read as follows:

```ts
import { NestFactory } from '@nestjs/core';
import { AppModule } from './app.module';

async function bootstrap() {
  const app = await NestFactory.create(AppModule, {
    bodyParser: true,
    rawBody: true,
  });
  app.enableCors();
  await app.listen(3000);
}
bootstrap();
```

Install Dependencies

We need to install stripe and dotenv.

```
npm i stripe dotenv
```

Env

Add the stripe secret key to the **.env** file

```
STRIPE_SECRET_KEY=sk_test_51K...
```

Stripe Module

Create a new module for stripe as follows:
```
nest generate resource modules/stripe
```
Select the option **REST API** and **no** for CRUD.

StripeService

Now we have StripeService created, let's declare the
checkout method.
```
import { Injectable } from
'@nestjs/common';
import { config } from 'dotenv';

config();

@Injectable()
export class StripeService {
  async checkout(preorder, headers) {
    const stripe =
require('stripe')(`${process.env.STRIPE_
SECRET_KEY}`);
    const lineItems = [];

    // Fill line items
```

```javascript
    const session = await
stripe.checkout.sessions.create({
      payment_method_types: ['card'],
      line_items: lineItems,
      mode: 'payment',
      success_url: headers.origin +
'/success',
      cancel_url: headers.origin +
'/cancel',
      metadata: {
        preOrderId: preorder.id,
      },
    });

    return { id: session.id };
  }
}
```

The checkout method has two parameters: preorder and headers.

I have a preorder table where I store all the details of the order at the beginning of the checkout process. The data in this table is temporary, you can delete it after the order is completed. The second parameter, headers, contains details about the domain so that I can use origin to format the full URL for success and cancel. Stripe will redirect to these URLs after the payment process is complete. I have created two pages in the frontend application, one for success and one for failure. They will be redirected by Stripe.

The first thing we should do in the checkout method is to create a new stripe instance as follows:

```js
const stripe =
require('stripe')(`${process.env.STRIPE_
SECRET_KEY}`);
```

Next, we declare an array of `lineItems`. It's empty at the beginning, but we will fill it soon.

```js
const lineItems = [];
```

`lineItems` is mandatory for the Stripe checkout. Passing an empty array will result in the checkout process not starting and giving an error message that `lineItems` is mandatory.

The third step is to create the checkout session. We ask Stripe to create one for us and provide all the necessary details.

```js
    const session = await
stripe.checkout.sessions.create({
    payment_method_types: ['card'],
    line_items: lineItems,
    mode: 'payment',
    success_url: headers.origin +
'/success',
    cancel_url: headers.origin +
'/cancel',
    metadata: {
      preOrderId: preorder.id,
    },
  });
```

You can specify any user-defined properties in the metadata. I will add the preOrderId. Stripe will send us this metadata along with other details in the webhook events. We can then create the order object based on the preOrder details.

At the end, we return the session ID.
It will be used by Angular to load the Stripe form.

```
return { id: session.id };
```

Fill `lineItems`

Here is how to fill the lineItems.

```
    const items =
JSON.parse(preorder.items);
    items.forEach((item) => {
      const unit_amount =
Math.round(item.price * 100);
      const lineItem = {
        price_data: {
          currency: 'usd',
          product_data: {
            name: item.name,
            images: [item.imageUrl],
          },
          unit_amount,
        },
        quantity: item.quantity,
      };
      lineItems.push(lineItem);
```

```
  });
```

Here is the complete code of the StripeService class:

```
import { Injectable } from
'@nestjs/common';
import { config } from 'dotenv';

config();

@Injectable()
export class StripeService {
  async checkout(preorder, headers) {
    const stripe =
require('stripe')(`${process.env.STRIPE_
SECRET_KEY}`);
    const lineItems = [];

    const items =
JSON.parse(preorder.items);
    items.forEach((item) => {
      const unit_amount =
Math.round(item.price * 100);
      const lineItem = {
        price_data: {
          currency: 'usd',
          product_data: {
            name: item.name,
            images: [item.imageUrl],
          },
          unit_amount,
        },
```

```javascript
      quantity: item.quantity,
    };
    lineItems.push(lineItem);
  });

  const session = await
stripe.checkout.sessions.create({
    payment_method_types: ['card'],
    line_items: lineItems,
    mode: 'payment',
    success_url: headers.origin +
'/success',
    cancel_url: headers.origin +
'/cancel',
    metadata: {
      preOrderId: preorder.id,
    },
  });

  return { id: session.id };
  }
}
```

Checkout Endpoint

Let's create a new endpoint for the checkout process in the ProductsController.
It will have two parameters, the `cartItems` and the `headers`.

```javascript
  @Post('checkout')
```

```
  async Checkout(@Body('cartItems')
cartItems, @Headers() headers) {

    // ...

    return
this.stripeService.checkout(preOrder,
headers);
  }
```

In the checkout endpoint, we receive the cartItems from the frontend endpoint together with the headers.
We create a new preOrder object and pass it together with the headers to the checkout method. We then return the result to the frontend application.
The cartItems array we get from the frontend contains only two properties, the productId and the quantity.
I don't pass any other details from the frontend, I mean the product price, image, etc.
I read these details from the product table in the backend, based on the received product IDs. For security reasons I should not retrieve the price from the frontend.
Here is the complete code for the checkout endpoint:

```
@Post('checkout')
  async Checkout(@Body('cartItems')
cartItems, @Headers() headers) {
    const products = await
this.productsService.getProducts(
      cartItems.map((t) => t.id),
    );
```

```javascript
    if (products && products.length > 0)
{
      const itemsArr =
products.map((product) => ({
        id: product.id,
        name: product.title,
        price: product.price,
        imageUrl: product.imageUrl,
        quantity:
          cartItems.find((item) =>
item.id === product.id)?.quantity ?? 1,
      }));
      let total = 0;
      const userId = 1;
      itemsArr.forEach((item) => {
        total += Math.round(item.price *
item.quantity);
      });
      const preOrder = await
this.preOrdersService.create({
        items: JSON.stringify(itemsArr),
        orderDate: new Date(),
        total,
        userId,
      });
      return
this.stripeService.checkout(preOrder,
headers);
    } else throw new
NotFoundException('Products not
found!');
```

```
}
```

Remember to import the StripeModule in the Products Module.

```typescript
import { Module, forwardRef } from
'@nestjs/common';
import { ProductsService } from
'./products.service';
import { ProductsController } from
'./products.controller';
import { StripeModule } from
'src/modules/stripe/stripe.module';
import { OrdersModule } from
'../orders/orders.module';

@Module({
  imports: [forwardRef(() =>
StripeModule), forwardRef(() =>
OrdersModule)],
  controllers: [ProductsController],
  providers: [ProductsService],
  exports: [ProductsService],
})
export class ProductsModule {}
```

Frontend

Install the stripe dependency

```
npm install @stripe/stripe-js
```

Add the stripe key property to the environment object.

```
export const environment = {
  API_URL: 'http://localhost:3000',
  STRIPE_PK: 'pk_test_51K...',
};
```

Declare the checkout method in the productsService as follows:

```
checkout(items: any) {
    return this.http.post(
      environment.API_URL +
'/products/checkout',
      {
        items,
      },
      {
        headers: {
          'Content-Type':
'application/json',
        },
      }
    );
  }
```

It calls the checkout endpoint and passes the cartItems as the body of the post method.

Let's now switch to the shopping cart page and implement the `onCheckout` method. It is triggered when the user clicks on the **"Continue to Checkout"** button.

In the **cart.component.ts**:

```typescript
  async onCheckout() {
    const stripe = await
loadStripe(environment.STRIPE_PK);
    const cartItems = this.cartService
      .cart()
      .items.map((item) => ({ id:
item.id, quantity: item.quantity }));
    this.productsService
      .checkout(cartItems)
      .pipe(first())
      .subscribe({
        next: async (response) => {
          const session = response as
any;

          const result = await
stripe?.redirectToCheckout({
            sessionId: session.id,
          });

          if (result?.error) {
            console.log(result?.error);
          }
        },
        error: (response) => {
          if (response?.error) {

console.log(response?.error);
          }
        },
      });
```

```
}
```

We start by loading the Stripe object. For performance, it is better to import from `@stripe/stripe-js/`**pure** than from `@stripe/stripe-js`.

We then prepare the `cartItems` that we send to the backend server. We eliminate all properties of the items and only keep the ID and the quantity.

Finally, we can call up the ProductsService checkout and wait for the response. Once we have received the session ID from the backend, we ask Stripe to redirect to the checkout session.

Done

Congratulations! You have completed the checkout process successfully. Run the NestJS server - restart it if it was already running -. Run the angular application. Add some items to the cart and do the checkout.

Stripe test cards

In test mode, use card 4242 4242 4242 4242 to make a successful payment.
You can cancel the payment by clicking on the "Back" button in the Stripe form.

Webhooks

Even if the payment process is complete, our transactions are not finished yet.
After we have successfully collected the money from the user, they should receive the product.
Therefore, the backend should be informed about the status of the payment transactions. This is where webhooks come into play.
Stripe sends you all payment events via the registered webhooks.

Webhooks Endpoints

Create a new webhook endpoint on the Stripe dashboard.
Endpoint url: `https://min-shop.com/webhooks`
Events: `checkout.session.completed` and `payment_intent.succeeded`.
Now go to the backend application and create the endpoint webhooks.
I will use the `StripeController` for this. Go to **stripe.controller.ts** and modify it as follows:

```
import { Controller, Post,
RawBodyRequest, Headers, Req } from
'@nestjs/common';
import { StripeService } from
'./stripe.service';

@Controller('webhook')
```

```ts
export class StripeController {
  constructor(private readonly
stripeService: StripeService) {}

  @Post('')
  async webhook(@Req() req:
RawBodyRequest<Request>, @Headers()
headers) {
    let result: any = true;

    return result;
  }
}
```

Add the webhook secret key to the **.env** file.

```
STRIPE_SECRET_KEY=sk_test_51K...
```

STRIPE_WEBHOOK_SECRET_KEY=whsec_27a...

We use a test secret key for the webhook. You should replace it with the live secret key when you go live.

Here is the complete code of the webhook controller, **stripe.controller.ts**:

```ts
import { Controller, Headers, Post,
RawBodyRequest, Req } from
'@nestjs/common';
import { config } from 'dotenv';
config();

const stripe =
require('stripe')(`${process.env.STRIPE_
SECRET_KEY}`);
```

```typescript
const endpointSecret =
`${process.env.STRIPE_WEBHOOK_SECRET_KEY
}`;

@Controller('webhook')
export class StripeController {
  @Post('')
  async webhook(@Req() req:
RawBodyRequest<Request>, @Headers()
headers) {
    const sig =
headers['stripe-signature'];
    let result: any = true;
    let event;

    try {
      event =
stripe.webhooks.constructEvent(req.rawBo
dy, sig, endpointSecret);
    } catch (err) {
      return `Webhook Error:
${err.message}`;
    }

    switch (event.type) {
      case 'checkout.session.completed':
        break;
      case 'payment_intent.succeeded':
        break;
      default:
```

```
        console.log(`Unhandled event
type ${event.type}`);
    }
    return result;
  }
}
```

Local Listener

Stripe CLI will forward webhooks events to our development environment. Go to the developer dashboard, the test mode → webhooks, then add a local listener.

Follow the instructions:

- Download and install the Stripe CLI.
- Run the command `stripe login`
- Run the command `stripe listen --forward-to localhost:3000/webhook`

The instructions will give you a secret webhook key that you can use. Insert it into the **.env** file.

Start the NestJS application and the frontend application and perform the checkout. Stripe will trigger our webhook endpoint with various events.

Use `console.log` or launch the debugger to watch what's going on.

PaymentIntent

A PaymentIntent is an object that represents a payment attempt. It encapsulates the entire lifecycle of a payment, including its status, amount, currency and payment method.

The main idea is that we store the preOrder details in the `checkout.session.completed` event and retrieve it in the `payment_intent.succeeded` to complete the order.

We store the `paymentIntentId` and the `preOrderId` in the database. We get the `paymentIntentId` from the `event.data.object.payment_intent` and the `preOrderId` from `event.data.object.metadata.preOrderId`. Remember that we send the `preOrderId` in the `metadata` when we create the checkout session.

In the `payment_intent.succeeded` event, we get the details of the pre-order based on the `paymentIntentId`. Now we have all the information to create the order and send the product to the customer. As a final step, we can delete the temporary record from the preOrders table.

Business Logic

Here is the complete code of the webhook controller including the business logic:

```typescript
import {
  Controller,
  Headers,
  InternalServerErrorException,
  Post,
  RawBodyRequest,
  Req,
} from '@nestjs/common';
import { PaymentIntentsService } from
'src/modules/stripe/payment-intents.serv
ice';

import { config } from 'dotenv';
import { PreOrdersService } from
'src/modules/orders/pre-orders.service';
import { OrdersService } from
'src/modules/orders/orders.service';
config();

const stripe =
require('stripe')(`${process.env.STRIPE_
SECRET_KEY}`);
const endpointSecret =
`${process.env.STRIPE_WEBHOOK_SECRET_KEY
}`;

@Controller('webhook')
export class StripeController {
  constructor(
    private paymentIntentsService:
PaymentIntentsService,
```

```typescript
    private preOrdersService:
PreOrdersService,
    private orderService: OrdersService,
  ) {}

  @Post('')
  async webhook(@Req() req:
RawBodyRequest<Request>, @Headers()
headers) {
    const sig =
headers['stripe-signature'];
    let result: any = true;
    let event;

    try {
      event =
stripe.webhooks.constructEvent(req.rawBo
dy, sig, endpointSecret);
    } catch (err) {
      return `Webhook Error:
${err.message}`;
    }

    switch (event.type) {
      case 'checkout.session.completed':
        result = await
this.paymentIntentsService.createPayment
Intent(

event.data.object.payment_intent,
```

```
        event.data.object.metadata.preOrderId,
        );
        break;
      case 'payment_intent.succeeded':
        try {
          setTimeout(async () => {
            const paymentIntentSucceeded
= event.data.object;
            const paymentIntentObj =
              await
this.paymentIntentsService.findOneByPaym
entIntentId(

paymentIntentSucceeded.id,
              );
            if (paymentIntentObj) {
            const preOrder = await
this.preOrdersService.getPreOrder(

paymentIntentObj.preOrderId,
              );
              if (preOrder) {

this.orderService.create({
                orderDate: new Date(),
                total: preOrder.total,
                userId:
preOrder.userId,
                items: preOrder.items,
```

```
                    paymentIntentId:
paymentIntentObj.paymentIntentId,
                });
                await
this.paymentIntentsService.delete(

paymentIntentObj.paymentIntentId,
                );
                await
this.preOrdersService.delete(preOrder.id
);
              } else {
              throw new
InternalServerErrorException('Pre Order
not found!');
              }
            } else {
            throw new
InternalServerErrorException(
                'Payment intent not
found!',
              );
            }
          }, 2000);
        } catch (e) {
          console.log('ERROR PAYMENT
SUCCESS: ', e);
        }
        break;
      default:
```

```
        console.log(`Unhandled event
type ${event.type}`);
    }
    return result;
  }
}
```

Cycle Completes

This completes the entire payment cycle. If we get the `checkout.session.completed` event, it means that the user has started paying and is completing the purchase in earnest. We create a `preOrder` object and store it along with the `paymentIntent` details.
When we receive the `payment_intent.succeeded` event, the money has already been received in our Stripe account and the payment has been successfully completed. We can release the product to the customer and save the order object in the database along with any further notifications or operations.

Now, stripe is complete, what we do when we get these events are business details.

Go Live

To go live, replace the test keys in the backend, frontend, and webhook with the live keys. That's all. You

don't need to make any further changes. All checkouts
are now real money and will land in your Stripe account.
Good luck!

Code Samples

Visit `https://books.abdelfattah-ragab.com` to
download the code samples.
After you have downloaded and unpacked the archive,
you will find two folders for Before and After.
The Before folder contains the first projects without
Stripe. The After folder contains the final projects after
we have integrated Stripe.
You should use your Stripe keys to make the Stripe
applications work.

Conclusion

Congratulations! You have read the book "Stripe Integration in Angular: A Step-by-Step Guide to Creating Payment Functionality". Now you are able to handle all payments scenarios with ease. Remember that learning Angular is an ongoing process. Practice makes perfect — build your own projects, experiment with the features you have learned, and delve into the extensive online resources.

Thank you for joining me in my exploration of Angular. I wish you the best of luck on your programming journey. Have fun programming and good luck with your applications!

Media Attributions

Gradient m logo template collection
Image by pikisuperstar on Freepik

Modern annual report magazine page flyer a company catalog
Image by starline on Freepik

Flat woman paying by pos terminal and refund cashback
Image by redgreystock on Freepik

Don't miss out!

Receive an email when Abdelfattah Ragab publishes a new book. It's free and without obligation.

Also by Abdelfattah Ragab

- ◇ Shippo Integration in Angular
- ◇ Responsive Layouts: Flex, Grid and Multi-Column
- ◇ Angular HTTP
- ◇ Angular Shopping Store

About the Author

Abdelfattah Ragab is a professional software developer with more than 20 years of experience.
https://abdelfattah-ragab.com

About the Publisher

Abdelfattah Ragab is a highly qualified and experienced software developer with over 20 years of experience in the industry. Specializing in front-end development, Abdelfattah Ragab has a deep understanding of Angular, JavaScript, TypeScript, HTML and CSS. Read more at https://abdelfattah-ragab.com